CHOPIN
MAZURKA in F MINOR
Opus Posthumous

Reconstructed and Edited by Kingsley Day
Recorded by Michael Mizrahi

On the cover:
A Salon in the Hotel of Monsieur Basile Parent,
Place Vendome, Paris, 1866 (oil on panel)
by Charles Giraud (1819–1892)
© Private Collection / The Bridgeman Art Library International

ISBN 978-1-4584-1439-7

G. SCHIRMER, Inc.

DISTRIBUTED BY
HAL•LEONARD®
CORPORATION
7777 W. BLUEMOUND RD. P.O. BOX 13819 MILWAUKEE, WI 53213

www.schirmer.com
www.halleonard.com

CONTENTS

PREFACE

When Frédéric Chopin died on October 17, 1849, he left behind a confusing one-page sketch for a mazurka in F minor. His pupil Jane Stirling and his close friend Auguste Franchomme (the cellist to whom he dedicated his Cello Sonata) both later wrote that the piece was composed at Chopin's rue de Chaillot address in Paris—the apartment where he lived in the summer of 1849. If so, the work was most likely his last completed composition, and it is often referred to as such. Having written the sketch, however, Chopin never took his usual next step of making a fair copy, whether because of failing health or an excess of self-criticism.

In a letter dated June 18, 1852, Stirling referred to the mazurka as a work "that everyone believed to be indecipherable" in telling Chopin's sister that Franchomme had in fact deciphered it. His copy presents the mazurka as a short piece in ABA form, and it was in this form that another of Chopin's close associates—his former copyist, Julian Fontana—prepared the work for publication. The mazurka was issued in 1855 as the composer's Op. 68, No. 4, and this 62-bar version is the one that has appeared in subsequent collections of the complete Chopin mazurkas.

Franchomme's copy and Fontana's edition, however, omit an entire section of Chopin's sketch, admittedly the section most difficult to unravel. In 1951 British musicologist Arthur Hedley had an opportunity to view the autograph sketch, then in private hands, and made the first attempt to reconstruct this additional 32-bar section. His version of the piece was privately circulated and occasionally performed but never published during his lifetime. Polish musicologist Ludwik Bronarski also had an opportunity to examine the sketch, and in two journal articles—published in 1955 and 1961—he transcribed the omitted section, though he declined to present a reconstruction of the entire mazurka.

In 1958 Chopin's sketch and Franchomme's copy were purchased by the Chopin Museum of Warsaw, where they were examined by Polish musicologist Jan Ekier. The result, issued by Polskie Wydawnictwo Muzyczne in 1965, was the first published edition of what purported to be the entire work, in ABACA form (Ekier's version was soon recorded by pianist Arthur Rubinstein in his 1967 set of the complete Chopin mazurkas). Although Ekier corrects significant errors in the

Fontana edition, he notates the previously omitted C section as 16 bars rather than 32, omitting at least two passages of Chopin's sketch—as can be seen by examining his edition's appended facsimile of the sketch.

In his 1973 article "Die letzte Inspiration des Meisters" (The Last Inspiration of the Master), published in the *Archiv für Musikwissenschaft,* Polish musicologist Wojciech Nowik (who had previously analyzed the sketch in a 1969 article) transcribes every fragment of music in Chopin's sketch and then offers a literal reconstruction of the piece, not as a performing edition but as a summary of his research conclusions. His version of the C section—though different from Ekier's version—is also 16 bars in length. It is followed by a return of the B section and then a final return of A, resulting in an overall form of ABACBA (though the second A section is only four bars long).

A 1975 edition by British pianist Ronald Smith, published by Hansen House, follows Ekier's ABACA structure but includes material Ekier had omitted from the C section, notating it as 32 bars. Smith's edition is no longer in print.

In 1983 Editions Concertino of Paris published a new reconstruction of the piece by Polish pianist and composer Milosz Magin, who recorded the complete works of Chopin for Decca. Magin's version is structurally identical to Smith's but differs from both the Smith and Ekier editions in many details.

In his article "Chopin's Last Style" (to which I am indebted for much of the information in this preface), published in the summer 1985 issue of the *Journal of the American Musicological Society,* American musicologist Jeffrey Kallberg reviews these and other developments and (in addition to contending that the work was written earlier than 1849 and thus was not Chopin's last composition) proposes that the mazurka's complete form is neither ABA nor ABACA but ABACABA. He also notes that even the more complete Smith and Magin versions fail to account for a puzzling passage in the sketch: a one-bar bass line that Chopin labeled *3ci.* Kallberg's article includes his transcriptions of three passages from the sketch but not a complete reconstruction of the work. (The article was republished with slight emendations as a chapter in Kallberg's 1996 book *Chopin at the Boundaries: Sex, History, and Musical Genre.*)

He discusses the mazurka further—reiterating that its form is ABACABA—in his essay "The Problem of Repetition and Return in Chopin's Mazurkas," published in the 1988 book *Chopin Studies,* edited by Jim Samson.

In 1986 Oxford University Press published *Chopin: A Selection,* edited by British pianist John Vallier, who in 1958 had given the first concert and broadcast performances of the unpublished Arthur Hedley reconstruction. This anthology includes Vallier's edition of Hedley's version: a reconstruction in ABACABA form (although the final A is abbreviated) that presents the C section as 32 bars and even finds a place for the 3*ci* one-measure bass line. In the C section, however, Hedley and Vallier include sketch material that Chopin had clearly crossed out. *Chopin: A Selection* is no longer in print.

In 2007, with Ekier as lead editor, the new *Polish National Edition of the Works of Fryderyk Chopin* reissued his version of the mazurka. Ekier alters two minor details from his 1965 edition; but despite more recent reconstructions with 32-bar C sections, he still contends that the C section is only 16 bars long. In his view, the passages he omits were trial balloons that Chopin did not intend to include in the completed piece. Chopin crossed out other passages in the sketch, however, and did not cross out the C-section passages that Ekier omits. Magin notes of Ekier's edition that "the central section, reconstructed as 16 measures, seemed too short relative to the whole. We know that Chopin had a very acute sense of the balance of musical form; thus the return of the principal theme, after these 16 measures, seemed to come too soon." Smith goes even further, contending that Ekier's edition "takes a disastrous short-cut in the F major episode."

In Kallberg's words, "Numerous attempts have been made to decipher the document, none entirely successful." Ekier built on the work of Hedley and Bronarski; Smith and Magin in turn wrote their versions in response to Ekier. As the most recent in this chronology, I am indebted to all of those who have previously tackled this musical conundrum, particularly Vallier, Kallberg, Magin, Smith, Nowik, Ekier, and Hedley. My version differs significantly from any previous reconstruction in several respects: length (with a return of the full ABA section after the C section, the total length is 158 measures); the inclusion of alternate readings for disputed passages; and new interpretations of the right-hand rhythm in the penultimate measure of the C section, the transition from C back to A, and the 3*ci* bass line (see notes for measures 77 and 93, measures 94–95, and measures 157–58, respectively).

In terms of details, I have heeded an observation made by Kallberg in an article for *Early Music:* "Chopin viewed

his sketches as private documents whose notation need make sense only to him." For Chopin, sketches were a quickly notated shorthand to remind him of what he had composed at the piano, and thus he sometimes notated chords incompletely and inadvertently omitted accidentals simply because, as the work's composer, he already knew which notes to play. (Indeed, it was not uncommon for Chopin to forget to indicate accidentals even in his fair copies; as he admitted to Fontana when sending him manuscripts for two nocturnes, "Perhaps they lack still flats or sharps.")

My hope is that the resulting edition makes sense both musicologically and musically. Given Chopin's penchant for revising his compositions even after they were published, there is no doubt that had he had the opportunity and inclination to continue working on the F minor Mazurka, he would have made changes to what he had notated in the sketch; but (as previous transcribers would no doubt agree) the sketch as deciphered stands on its own as a complete musical work, one fully worthy of a place in the composer's oeuvre. Some have contended that the piece survives only as a sketch because Chopin was dissatisfied with it and thus intentionally chose not to prepare it for publication. Even if so, however, I join with transcribers from Franchomme to the present day who would disagree with such a self-critical appraisal. This mazurka is indisputably the work of a genius, and as such it deserves to be heard as fully and accurately as possible.

For their encouragement and support at various stages of this project, I am grateful to Duffie Adelson, president, Merit School of Music; D. J. Hoek, head, Northwestern University Music Library; Marjory Irvin, professor emerita of piano and theory, Lawrence University; Gayle Kowalchyk, senior keyboard editor, Alfred Publishing; Barbara Kreader, keyboard consultant for educational keyboard publications, Hal Leonard Corporation, and contributing editor, *Clavier Companion*; Jane Magrath, Grant Endowed Chair in Piano and Regents Professor, University of Oklahoma; Robert McDonald, piano faculty, Juilliard School, and Penelope P. Watkins Chair in Piano Studies, Curtis Institute of Music; Phillip Moll, professor for song interpretation, College of Music and Theater, Leipzig; Marie Rolf, associate dean of graduate studies and professor of music theory, Eastman School of Music; my dear friend Mark Weston; and especially Richard Walters, vice president of classical and vocal publications, and Joshua Parman, classical editor, Hal Leonard Corporation. Most of all I thank Jeffrey Kallberg, associate dean for arts and letters and professor of music history at the University of Pennsylvania, for his encouragement and for so generously sharing his insights and expertise.

—Kingsley Day

EDITORIAL NOTES

In endeavoring to make this edition as complete, accurate, and musically convincing as possible, I have diverged in several significant respects from the conclusions presented in previous reconstructions of Chopin's sketch. Although I hope the following comments justify my choices, the performer has the option of adopting as alternative readings any of the differing interpretations cited in the examples below.

All measure numbers refer to the present edition.

M. 1

The first published edition as prepared by Julian Fontana includes the initial tempo indication "Andantino," but there is no tempo marking in either Chopin's sketch or Auguste Franchomme's copy.

MM. 2, 4, 6

Most editors indicate that the turn in measure 2 and the trills in measures 4 and 6 are to be played identically: as two short notes (the principal note and the note above) beginning on the beat. Traditionally, however (as in recordings by such artists as Arthur Rubinstein, Vladimir Ashkenazy, Arturo Benedetti Michelangeli, and Evgeny Kissin), these two notes are played before the beat. (The same interpretive decisions apply to measures 41, 43, and 45; measures 97, 99, and 101; and measures 136, 138, and 140.)

M. 39

Chopin's sketch gives two versions of the left hand of this measure: a simpler version and, on the staff immediately below it, a somewhat more elaborate version. Although Chopin often wrote variants of particular passages, he typically wrote them when revisiting a given piece—for instance, when preparing a parallel edition of a composition for a publisher in a different country (see the chapter "The Chopin 'Problem': Simultaneous Variants and Alternate Versions" in Jeffrey Kallberg's *Chopin at the Boundaries: Sex, History, and Musical Genre* for a thorough discussion of this issue). Editors of Chopin may include these variants as ossia, but Chopin himself—unlike, for example, Rachmaninoff—was not in the habit of providing ossia passages. In fact, to all appearances the two versions of this measure's

left hand were notated at the same time; there is no discontinuity in ink shade or density to indicate that the second version was added as a later variant of the first. So the most likely explanation for these two left-hand options is that the piece's B section is heard twice, first with one version (measure 39) and later with the other (measure 134). A return of the B section means that the work's overall form—as first proposed (albeit for different reasons) by Kallberg in his 1985 article "Chopin's Last Style" in the *Journal of the American Musicological Society*—is ABACABA, rather than ABA as in Franchomme and Fontana or ABACA as in reconstructions by Jan Ekier, Ronald Smith, and Milosz Magin. For that matter, on the basis of Chopin's sketch, it is every bit as logical to assume that the C section is followed by a return of ABA as that it is followed by a return of A alone. The Arthur Hedley–John Vallier edition adopts these same conclusions, presenting the piece in ABACABA form and using the simpler version of this left-hand passage at the end of the first B section and the more elaborate version at the end of the second B section. (Their edition truncates the final return of A, however, on the grounds that Chopin often did so. Chopin more often did not do so, and to me their abrupt jump within the final A section seems unconvincing.)

MM. 63–93

Within the A and B sections of the sketch, the sequence of material is relatively clear; but the C section as sketched is a confusing grab bag of musical fragments, some connected by lines, others crossed out. No wonder Franchomme and Fontana failed to reconstruct it.

The Hedley-Vallier version includes material that is clearly crossed out in the sketch, while Ekier omits passages that clearly are not crossed out. By contrast, the two remaining post-Fontana editions, by Smith and Magin, include all of the C-section material—up to the transition back to A—that was not struck out and none of the material that was. In the process they present the sequence of passages in the C section identically. Although no ordering of this section's material can be adopted with absolute certainty, their solution makes sense to me both musically and in terms of fidelity to the sketch.

MM. 77, 93

In the sketch, the right hand of this measure appears to consist of five eighth notes followed by a quarter note with a fermata.

Previous reconstructions have interpreted this in one of two ways: in Ekier, Nowik, and Hedley-Vallier as six eighth notes (Kallberg notes in private correspondence that in sketches, Chopin often failed to fully extend beams),

or per Smith, Magin, and Kallberg's "Chopin's Last Style," as two eighths, an eighth-note triplet figure, and a quarter note.

If the final note is an eighth (as in the second of the three preceding examples), to my ear the fermata over the last note makes no musical sense. Ekier apparently agrees, but his solution is to omit the fermata even though it clearly appears in the sketch. If the last note is a quarter note, as it indeed appears to be, that leaves five eighth notes occupying the two preceding quarter-note beats, and so logically three of them might constitute a triplet. But which three? Smith and Magin presumably follow the measure's vertical alignment; the third eighth (D) is almost directly above the second left-hand quarter note, so they interpret that D as the start of the triplet. The result (in the third of the preceding examples), however, sounds more than a bit awkward.

But in other passages of the sketch consisting of right-hand eighth notes over left-hand quarter notes (e.g., measures 16–18), Chopin pays no attention to vertical alignment whatsoever. This suggests that in measure 77 the first three eighths could just as easily be a triplet, and I find this option musically superior to either of the preceding interpretations. Since the passage occurs twice (in measures 77 and 93), the fermata logically falls only in the second iteration, as in the Magin and Hedley-Vallier editions.

M. 88

In terms of individual pitches, I, like all who have previously tried to decipher this piece, have had to rely on intelligent guesswork to a much greater extent in the C section than in the preceding sections. Perhaps the most puzzling spot of all is the second beat of this measure; below the melody note is a quarter note floating below the staff, and in front of that note is an ink blot. Previous editors have notated this measure as either

but to my ear neither sounds persuasive; toggling from B-flat to B-natural back to B-flat seems harmonically weak, and a noncadential 4-3 suspension sounds out of character in the context of this piece. Interpreting the right hand of this measure as identical to that of measure 80 would make musical sense but would result in a B-flat as the low note of the third-beat chord, and in the sketch that note is unambiguously a B-natural. My best guess as to the lower note on the second beat is C-sharp, which actually makes sense if the chords are filled out (as I and previous transcribers have done with other chords in the C section) by adding an A-sharp on the second beat and a D on the third beat. This chromaticism seems appropriate in the context of this particular phrase, already the most chromatic in the entire piece.

MM. 94–95

In Chopin's sketch, the two measures at the end of the double-staff fragment labeled *F dur* most likely form the end of the first half of the C section (measures 77–78). After the various insertions and repetitions that constitute the C section's second half, these two measures return to close the C section as a whole. But although the first half of this two-bar passage functions just as aptly the second time as it does the first time, the same cannot be said of the second of the two bars; as written, it would lead to yet another return of the C-section opening, and instead it needs to lead back to a return of the A section. Of course the bass F on the first beat of the measure is not a problem in this regard, and apparently Chopin assumed that this bass note would indeed be heard again as the downbeat of measure 94. As a replacement right hand for the measure this second time around, he notated a one-measure passage, presumably in treble clef, directly above the earlier version.

The Ekier, Smith, and Magin reconstructions thus notate the transition from C back to A along these lines:

But roughly below the left hand of this same measure in the sketch, Chopin wrote the following:

The Hedley-Vallier edition thus eschews an immediate resolution of measure 93's dominant seventh chord and notates the transition from C back to A as

The three editors who adopt the right-hand option omit the left-hand measure entirely from their reconstructions; Hedley and Vallier, conversely, completely omit the right-hand measure and the downbeat bass note F that presumably would accompany it.

Assuming that both these added measures should be accounted for, a further option presents itself. Perhaps Chopin wrote the right-hand measure as his initial attempt at this transition but then felt that the shift from F major back to F minor was too abrupt. So perhaps he then followed that measure with the left-hand measure of repeated Cs, mentally transposing the C quarter-note pickup at the end of the previous measure down an octave so that it is in the same octave as the new passage. The result is the reading in this edition's measures 94–95.

MM. 157–58

At the end of the A section as notated at the beginning of Chopin's sketch, the last two bars are followed by the indication *F dur,* meaning that these bars are to be followed by the passage (the beginning of the C section) that Chopin so labels later in the sketch. Immediately below these two measures is an alternate two-measure ending for the A section: the ending that leads to the B section, which follows it immediately on the staff below. Kallberg, in his chapter "The Problem of Repetition and Return in Chopin's Mazurkas" in *Chopin Studies* (edited by Jim Samson), persuasively explains why these endings are in the wrong order—why the ending that leads to B is spatially preceded by the ending that leads to C. The first of the two endings is actually notated as follows:

As Kallberg observes, this passage was originally intended as the transition to Chopin's first attempt at a contrasting section, one notated starting at the far left side of the page immediately below the A section. This first attempt proved abortive, however, and is crossed out; Chopin tried again a little further down the sheet (again starting on the far left side of the page) but crossed out that false start as well. Directly below that second attempt (and, yet again, starting on the far left side of the page) is his third attempt, the passage labeled *F dur.* This spatial sequence convinces Kallberg that the initial form of the piece was (using labels corresponding to the work's final shape) ACA. Only later did Chopin expand the A section into an ABA complex, obliging him to write a new ending to the A section so as to lead to B. (As further spatial confirmation of this hypothesis, the B section that begins immediately below this new ending is written entirely on the right half of the page.) Because the *F dur* section begins with a quarter-note pickup, the final beat of the initially written A-section ending (above) is superseded and thus, although not crossed out, should clearly be omitted.

Immediately to the right of the sketch's second-to-be-composed ending is the bass line only of a third ending for the A section, and—as Kallberg points out—it is even labeled as such: *3ci,* meaning *trzeci* (Polish for "third"). Ekier, Smith, and Magin omit this cryptic passage entirely.

Significantly, Chopin writes the beam connecting the four eighth notes so that it continues upward and to the right, past the stem of the last eighth note, and places an ascending slur over the four eighth notes that also extends past the last stem. This measure is written in lighter, thinner ink strokes than the rest of the sketch, possibly indicating that it was added later than the adjacent passages.

Kallberg, in his "Chopin's Last Style," interprets this passage as literally notated and, given the inconclusiveness of the last note (D-flat), surmises that this ending leads into another section of the work; he takes this as evidence that the B section recurs after the third A section (and thus that the piece's overall form is ABACABA). Nowik's reconstruction does indeed include the passage as a transition from A to B, although he appends the A section's first (spatially second) ending as an alternate version of this transition. In order for this even to begin to make musical sense, Nowik is obliged to use the right hand of the second (spatially first) ending of A, thus omitting from measure 118 the two right-hand pickup eighth notes (G and A-flat) that clearly begin the B theme in the sketch.

And even with this questionable omission, the D-flat at the end of the measure steals much of the thunder of a harmonic progression between two chords (F minor and E-flat seventh) that share no common tones.

As Ekier has pointed out in another context, "Mistakes in the number of ledger lines are among the most frequently made by Chopin and occurred throughout his life." Hedley and Vallier (whose edition is the only previous published version to present the piece as ABACABA) conclude that the D-flat is really an F with a missing second ledger line and then do in fact use the sketch's first A-to-B transition the first time and the *3ci* passage as the transition from A to B the second time.

Kallberg has suggested in private correspondence that if the D-flat is indeed a notational error (perhaps "a hurried last stroke of the pen," as he says of a puzzling final note in another Chopin sketch), a much more likely reading is C. With the D-flat changed to a C, the *3ci* passage can indeed function quite satisfactorily as a second transition from A to B.

However, I have searched Chopin's sectional dances (the mazurkas, polonaises, and waltzes) for instances where an A section is followed immediately by a B section and then, later in the piece, the A section returns intact and is again followed immediately by B (in B's original key). I found not one single such case where the second A-to-B transition differs from the first. Where post-A transitions differ are those cases (as in the Mazurka in B Major, Op. 56, No. 1) where A leads in one instance to a B section and in a later instance to a C section—just as in the mazurka under discussion. Thus the likelihood that Chopin would use two different A-to-B transitions here seems slim, especially given that the second of the two options is less interesting harmonically than the first. Assuming, then, that the first A ending recurs at the end of the first A in the reprise of the ABA complex (i.e., that measure 118 is identical to measure 23), it seems conceivable that in the context of a sketch, Chopin would not have regarded that internal "ending" (within a repeat of a three-section complex) as needing to be numbered. In such a case, the A ending that he labeled as the third *(3ci)* would most plausibly be the ending for the second iteration of ABA—labeled *3ci* simply because it is the third of the three notated endings—and thus the end of the entire piece. If the piece is indeed in ABACABA form, then, as I interpret it, the third

(3ci) ending is literally the ending of the fourth A; but given that in other Chopin sketches, endings are rarely if ever numbered, and third (much less fourth) endings are rare if not nonexistent, unorthodox numbering of endings here does not seem all that improbable. In any case, in this reconstruction, the sketch's last notated ending is the ending of the last A.

Squeezing this bass-clef ending into the small space at the end of the third stave, Chopin writes a quarter note and four eighth notes, with the ascending eighth-note beam and the accompanying ascending slur—the only slur in the entire sketch—extending past the last note. These details strike me as shorthand for an arpeggio that keeps going up. If, as Kallberg suggests, the D-flat could be interpreted as a misnotated C, and if the arpeggio does indeed continue upward to conclude with the tonic F on the downbeat of the next measure, the result is a more final, differentiated ending than what would otherwise be a simple, perfunctory *Fine* after the first two beats of the ABA segment's last measure (as in Smith and Magin, below).

The D-flat in the *3ci* passage might be accurate if Chopin intended to end the piece along these lines:

But in these versions, the resolution of D-flat to C is the most crucial musical gesture; and, given how crucial it is, surely Chopin would have actually notated it, by writing a C after the D-flat, instead of merely hinting, via the extended beam, that the figure continues. True, he had run out of space at the end of the line; but elsewhere in the sketch he extends the staff lines by hand to add material, as he could easily have done here.

Again I cite Kallberg's *Chopin Studies* chapter, where he observes that over the course of his career Chopin became increasingly concerned with giving his mazurkas more definite conclusions rather than just stopping them abruptly at the end of the final return of A. In several cases the result of this concern was an elaborate coda; certainly, by comparison, a rising tonic arpeggio seems somewhat routine, but at least it is less routine than no special ending at all.

Mazurka in F Minor
Opus Posthumous (Originally Published as Op. 68, No. 4)

Fingering by Michael Mizrahi

Frédéric Chopin
Reconstructed by Kingsley Day

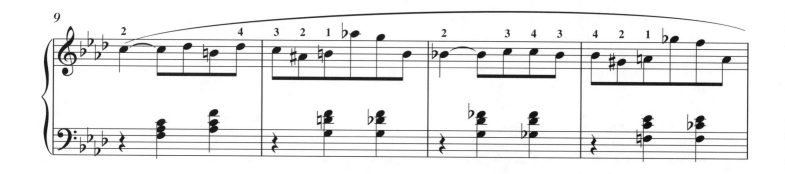

All dynamics, tempo indications, phrase markings, pedaling, and fingerings are editorial,
as there are none in Chopin's sketch.
Small noteheads indicate editorial estimations of the intended content.

ABOUT THE RECORDING ARTIST

Michael Mizrahi

Pianist Michael Mizrahi has won acclaim for his compelling performances of a wide-ranging repertoire and his ability to connect with audiences of all ages. He has appeared as concerto soloist, recitalist, chamber musician, and teaching artist across the United States and abroad.

Dr. Mizrahi has performed in the world's leading concert halls including Carnegie Hall, Toyko's Suntory Hall, the Kimmel Center in Philadelphia, Jordan Hall and the Gardner Museum in Boston, the Kennedy Center in Washington, DC, the Chicago Cultural Center, and Houston's Jones Hall. He has performed as soloist with major orchestras including the Houston Symphony, National Symphony, Haddonfield Symphony, Sioux City Symphony, and Prince Georges Philharmonic. He has given solo recitals at the Phillips Collection in Washington, DC, and has made repeated appearances on the Dame Myra Hess Concert Series in Chicago. His chamber music festival appearances include Music@ Menlo, Verbier, the Yellow Barn Music Festival, and the Steans Institute at the Ravinia Festival. Dr. Mizrahi won First Prize and the Audience Choice Award in the Ima Hogg International Competition, as well as first prizes in the International Bartók-Kabalevsky Competition and the Iowa International Piano Competition. He won third prize in the San Antonio International Piano Competition in 2006. Dr. Mizrahi appeared for many years on the active roster of Astral Artists.

Dedicated to the music of our time, Dr. Mizrahi has commissioned and given world premieres of several new works for piano and frequently collaborates with composers and instrumentalists in the performance of 21st-century music. He is a founding member of NOW Ensemble, a chamber group devoted to the commissioning and performing of new music by emerging composers. NOW Ensemble released its second album, *Awake*, to critical acclaim in 2011. Dr. Mizrahi will release an album of newly commissioned works for solo piano on the New Amsterdam Records label in spring 2012.

An enthusiastic promoter of music education, Mizrahi has presented lecture-recitals and master classes at The American School in Switzerland (TASIS), the University of North Carolina at Wilmington, and the University of Nebraska at Omaha. As a member of Carnegie Hall's prestigious Academy program and Teaching Artists Collaborative from 2007 to 2009, Dr. Mizrahi spent several hours a week as a teaching artist in New York City public schools.

Dr. Mizrahi is also a founding member of the Moët Trio, which is quickly establishing itself as one of today's most exciting young piano trios. The Moët Trio recently completed a residency at the New England Conservatory.

Michael Mizrahi received his bachelor's degree from the University of Virginia, where his concentrations were in music, religion, and physics. He holds masters and doctoral degrees from the Yale School of Music, where he studied with Claude Frank. After his Philadelphia debut recital, the *Philadelphia Inquirer* wrote that "...the performance had transparency, revealing a forward-moving logic and chord voices you didn't previously realize were there...textures were sumptuous." He is currently assistant professor of piano at Lawrence University in Appleton, Wisconsin.

ABOUT THE EDITOR

Kingsley Day

Kingsley Day is active in the Chicago area as a writer, editor, composer, and performer. No stranger to rescuing obscure scores, he produced a new performing edition of the piano-vocal score for the 1917 Jerome Kern musical *Oh, Boy!* as pianist-music director for its recent Chicago revival and composed a new score for Gilbert and Sullivan's lost operetta *Thespis* that has received three Chicago-area productions. His *Thespis* score was hailed by the *Chicago Tribune* as "an inspired substitute in the Sullivan style" and "the genuine article, music that would do credit to the master himself."

Since 1993 Day has been a senior editor at Northwestern University. Previously he served for five years as the editor of *Clavier* magazine. His publications have won multiple awards from the Council for the Advancement and Support of Education and the Educational Press Association.

Day has written the music and lyrics and cowritten the books for a number of musicals that have been successfully produced in the Chicago area and beyond. Among these is *Summer Stock Murder*, winner of a Joseph Jefferson Award for new work in its first production at Stage 773 and subsequently produced in the Chicago area at Drury Lane Oakbrook and across the country and abroad as part of the Rodgers & Hammerstein Theatricals catalog. He also cowrote the comedy *Tour de Farce*, which has been produced twice in Chicago, twice in the greater New York City area, and at theaters across the United States and Europe. With his theatrical collaborator Philip LaZebnik, Day

was twice awarded a grant by the Paul and Gabriela Rosenbaum Foundation's New Musicals Project.

Active in professional theater for more than three decades, Day has served as pianist-music director for productions at such Chicago-area venues as the Apollo Theater, Stage 773, the onetime Drury Lane Evergreen Park, and City Lit Theater, for which he recently composed new incidental music for Ben Jonson's *Volpone.* A two-time Jeff Award nominee as pianist-music director for the late lamented National Jewish Theater from 1988 to 1996, he arranged the scores for the company's five original full-length revues spotlighting the songs of Kurt Weill, Irving Berlin, Richard Rodgers, George Gershwin, and Frank Loesser. Day has also appeared onstage as a singer-actor in productions by Light Opera Works, City Lit Theater, Porchlight Music Theatre, Bailiwick Repertory Theater, Theater Wit, the Chicago Premiere Society, the Chicago Gilbert & Sullivan Society, and the Savoyaires. For three summer seasons he appeared as a music director, pianist, and actor at Cortland Repertory Theatre in upstate New York. As a solo and chamber music pianist, Day performs regularly on the First Congregational Church of Evanston's Robinson Recital Series, for which he is also the program annotator.

Day graduated magna cum laude from Lawrence University with a bachelor of music in piano as a student of Theodore Rehl. He completed his master of arts and ABD in music theory at the Eastman School of Music, where he studied piano with Maria Luisa Faini.